A *Doonesbury* book

Adjectives Will Cost You Extra

Selected Cartoons from
He's Never Heard of You, Either

G. B. Trudeau

FAWCETT CREST • NEW YORK

ADJECTIVES WILL COST YOU EXTRA

Adjectives Will Cost You Extra

HEY, ZONKER, YOU GOT AN OVERNIGHT BAG?

UNDER MY BED. YOU GOING SOMEWHERE?

WELL, IF I CAN TALK MIKE OUT OF HIS CAR, I'D LIKE TO GO HOME TOMORROW. IS HE AROUND?

IN THE KITCHEN. HE'S WORKING ON A DATE FOR NEW YEAR'S.

THE CONNALLY WAY OFFERS YOU THAT RESPECT. IT GIVES YOU THE SPACE IN WHICH TO REALIZE YOUR EARNING POTENTIAL. IT SAYS THAT TAX INCENTIVES ARE OKAY. AND BY DEREGULATING INDUSTRY, IT CREATES A CONTEXT FOR GROWTH.

I FEEL BETTER ABOUT MYSELF ALREADY.

ME, TOO.

WE CALL IT "GETTING YOURS."

WELL, YEAH, AS A MATTER OF FACT, I HAVE. IT CONCERNS ENVIRONMENTAL STANDARDS..
YES?

SOMETIMES I FANTASIZE ABOUT RELAX-ING THEM.
RELAXIN' 'EM? HELL, WHY NOT PUT 'EM TO SLEEP?
G B Trudeau

CHARGING THAT CARTER HAD UNFAIRLY TAKEN ADVANTAGE OF THE BAN BY RALLYING THE COUNTRY BEHIND HIM, CONNALLY SAID HE WAS "SICK AND TIRED OF PUTTING HOSTAGES AHEAD OF POLITICS."

THE CALL FOR DISUNITY IS EXPECTED TO RECEIVE BIPARTISAN SUPPORT.

NOW MORE THAN EVER, WE MUST NOT PERMIT OURSELVES TO BE OVERCOME WITH A NEW MISSILE MADNESS, A MINDLESS RENEWAL OF UNRESTRICTED COMPETITION.

BEFORE IT IS TOO LATE, WE MUST MOVE TO RATIFY SALT. SALT IS NOT A UNILATERAL FAVOR WE ARE DOING THE SOVIET UNION; WE SHOULD NOT BE PENALIZING OURSELVES FOR SOVIET BEHAVIOR!

GOOD EVENING. TODAY THE FIRST MAJOR SCANDAL OF THE '80's SWEPT THROUGH THE NATION'S CAPITAL LIKE A TIDAL WAVE. ROLAND HEDLEY WAS THERE.

THE NEWS HIT WASHINGTON LIKE A BOMBSHELL. CONGRESSIONAL INVESTIGATORS HAD LINKED ATTORNEY GENERAL BENJAMIN CIVILETTI TO THE LARGEST ENTRAPMENT SCANDAL IN U.S. HISTORY.

THE FULL SCOPE OF THE RING'S ACTIVITIES IS STILL UNKNOWN, BUT THE D.C. OPERATION IS THOUGHT TO BE ONLY PART OF A MASSIVE, NATIONWIDE SCHEME TO DISCREDIT AND SMEAR PROMINENT PUBLIC OFFICIALS.

FBI MOTIVES WERE UNCERTAIN. BACK AFTER THIS.

GBTrudeau

HOW DID THE LEGISLATORS GATHER ENOUGH EVIDENCE TO BUST UP THE FBI ENTRAPMENT RING? I ASKED ONE OF THE CONGRESSMEN INVOLVED..

PIECE OF CAKE, REALLY. I SIMPLY PUT OUT THE WORD I WAS OPEN TO A BRIBE. THE RUSE WORKED LIKE A CHARM. WITHIN DAYS, I WAS BEING HANDED $50,000 IN TAXPAYERS' MONEY!

IF THIS SCANDAL HAS A HERO, THEN SURELY IT IS ARMSTRONG ALGER, THE ONLY FBI AGENT TO REFUSE TO ENTRAP AN UNDERCOVER CONGRESSMAN. ALGER DESCRIBED THE ENCOUNTER TO ABC NEWS.

ACTUALLY IT WAS VERY BRIEF. HE SIMPLY TURNED UP AT THE HOUSE ONE NIGHT, SAID HE HAD HEARD ABOUT THE BRIBES AND WANTED A PIECE OF THE ACTION.

SO I'LL BE WORKING FROM PAPERS AND JOURNALS, IS THAT RIGHT?

A ROOM FULL. YOU BEEN IN THIS RACKET LONG?

LONG ENOUGH TO GHOST SEVEN AUTHORIZED MEMOIRS AND OVER TWENTY UNAUTHORIZED, INCLUDING THREE ON ELVIS. ALSO, I WAS THE BACKUP GHOST ON BOTH OF DAN RATHER'S BOOKS.

SO YOU THINK YOU'LL BE HITTING THE TALK SHOW CIRCUIT, ZEKE?

OH, FOR SURE, MAN. HELL, THAT'S THE BEST PART OF PUBLISHING A BOOK!

THE ACTUAL AUTHORING, THOUGH, IS SOMETHING ELSE. WRITING A BOOK REQUIRES PATIENCE, CONCENTRATION AND AN INCREDIBLE AMOUNT OF SELF-DISCIPLINE.